My Life as a

Christian

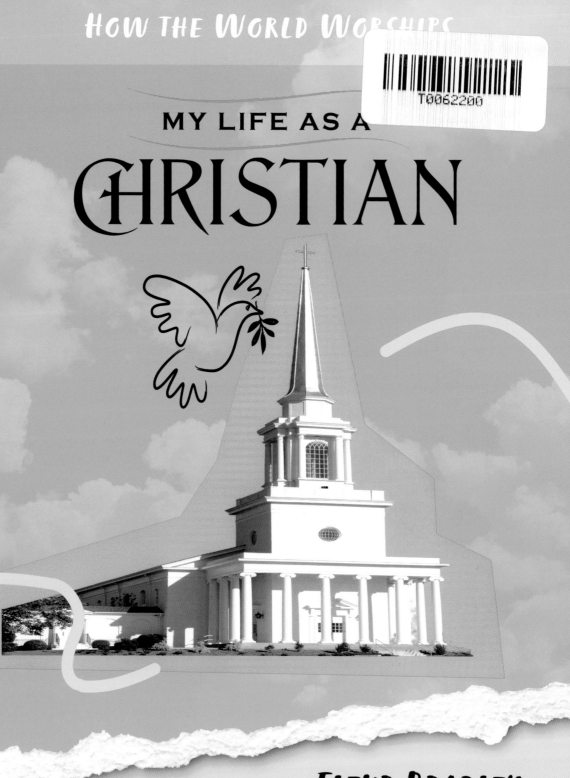

Fleur Bradley

45TH PARALLEL PRESS

Published in the United States of America by Cherry Lake Publishing Group
Ann Arbor, Michigan
www.cherrylakepublishing.com

Editorial Consultant: Dr. Virginia Loh-Hagan, EdD, Literacy, San Diego State University
Content Adviser: Molly H. Bassett, Associate Professor and Chair in the Department of Religious Studies
    at Georgia State University
Reading Adviser: Beth Walker Gambro, MS, Ed., Reading Consultant, Yorkville, IL
Book Designer: Jen Wahi

Photo Credits: © Sean Pavone/Shutterstock, cover, 1; © Marc Bruxelle/Shutterstock, 4; © mimagephotography/
    Shutterstock, 8; © TyronRoss/Shutterstock, 11; © Donald Linscott/Shutterstock, 12; © Kyle M Price/
    Shutterstock, 14; © Sahara Prince/Shutterstock, 16; © Revilo Lessen/Shutterstock, 17; © Iakov Filimonov/
    Shutterstock, 18; © Roock at Polish Wikipedia/Wikimedia, 21; Public Domain/Carnegie Museum of Art/
    Painted by Simon Bening/Acc. No. 64.11.6, 24; © Triff/Shutterstock, 27; © Andrij Vatsyk/Shutterstock, 28;
    © Manat Ratta/Shutterstock, 30

45th Parallel Press is an imprint of Cherry Lake Publishing Group.

Library of Congress Cataloging-in-Publication Data

Names: Bradley, Fleur, author.
Title: My life as a Christian / by Bradley, Fleur.
Description: Ann Arbor, MI : Cherry Lake Publishing, 2022. | Series: How the world worships |
    Includes bibliographical references.
Identifiers: LCCN 2021039842 | ISBN 9781534199408 (hardcover) | ISBN 9781668900543 (paperback) |
    ISBN 9781668906309 (ebook) | ISBN 9781668901984 (pdf)
Subjects: LCSH: Christianity—Juvenile literature.
Classification: LCC BR125.5 .F54 2022 | DDC 230—dc23
LC record available at https://lccn.loc.gov/2021039842

Printed in the United States of America
Corporate Graphics

ABOUT THE AUTHOR:

Fleur Bradley is originally from the Netherlands. She likes to travel and learn about different cultures whenever she can. Fleur has written many stories for kids and educational books. She now lives in Colorado with her family.

TABLE OF CONTENTS

INTRODUCTION 5

CHAPTER 1:
AN AMERICAN CHRISTIAN 9

CHAPTER 2:
REFLECTING ON MISSION WORK 15

CHAPTER 3:
A YOUNG CATHOLIC IN GERMANY 19

CHAPTER 4:
AN EASTER CELEBRATION 25

ACTIVITY: PAINTING EASTER EGGS 30

TIMELINE OF MAJOR EVENTS. 31

LEARN MORE 31

GLOSSARY. 32

INDEX 32

Did you know? Not much is known about Jesus's childhood. The Christian Bible mentions his birth. It also mentions a 12-year-old Jesus speaking to the Jewish teachers. Then the story of Jesus jumps to when he's 30.

Introduction

Religions are systems of faith and worship. Do you have a religion? About 80 percent of the world's population does. That's 4 out of 5 people.

Every religion is different. Some have one God. That's called **monotheism**. Other religions have multiple gods. This is called **polytheism**. Some religions have an **icon** instead of a god. An icon is an important figure. Christianity is a monotheistic religion.

Christianity is the world's largest religion. About 31 percent of people are Christian. More than 11 percent of all Christians live in the United States.

Christianity is based on the life and teachings of Jesus of Nazareth. He was believed to be born between 6 and 4 BCE in Judaea. Judaea is in the southern part of what is now Palestine.

During this time, Romans ruled Judaea. People feared the Romans. They feared their harsh punishments. Jesus was Jewish. He was considered a **rabbi** from a young age. A rabbi is a Jewish teacher, or priest. Jesus taught his followers to obey God's laws.

He taught them to love everyone. He also said that they should ask for God's forgiveness if they failed.

Many believed Jesus could perform miracles. They even thought he could raise the dead. Jewish leaders began to fear Jesus's power. They had him arrested. They took Jesus before the Roman authorities. Jesus was **crucified**. Crucified means to be nailed to a cross. He died.

Jesus's followers believed he was **resurrected**. Resurrected means raised from the dead. They believed Jesus was both human and divine. He became known as Jesus Christ. In Greek, **Christos** means "anointed one," or "Messiah." The life, death, and resurrection of Jesus Christ led to the creation of Christianity.

The Christian faith has many branches. The 2 largest branches are Catholics and Protestants. Catholicism is the oldest branch. Catholics have the Pope as their leader. Protestants do not see the Pope as their leader. They follow their **clergy** instead. Clergy are people trained to perform services in the church.

There are thousands of denominations within the Protestant faith. Denominations are branches of Christianity. The United States is home to many of those branches. Christians believe in a single God that includes 3 persons—the Father, Son, and Holy Spirit. This is called the **Holy Trinity**.

CATHOLIC POPE

There are "rankings" in the Catholic Church. There are deacons, priests, bishops, archbishops, cardinals, and the pope. The Pope is the "highest rank." The Pope is the spiritual leader of the Catholic Church. He lives in the Vatican in Rome. The Pope directs Catholics around the world.

Popes are elected during a papal conclave. A papal conclave is a time when the College of Cardinals comes together to choose a new Pope. This happens after a Pope passes away. Or more rarely, when a Pope resigns. Catholics believe that the Pope is the apostolic successor of Saint Peter. Apostolic succession means the spiritual authority of Jesus's 12 Apostles is passed on. Apostles are teachers of the Christian faith. This spiritual authority is passed on uninterrupted from Pope to Pope and bishop to bishop. *Saint* means "holy person." Saint Peter was 1 of Jesus's 12 apostles. Saint Peter was the first pope.

Maya
American Baptist

CHAPTER 1
AN AMERICAN CHRISTIAN

"Maya, watch out for that puddle!" Jonah calls from the construction site. Jonah is our youth group minister.

I laugh and nod. That was close—I almost tripped. Since I'm carrying boxes of nails, that would've been a mess. I'm on a **mission trip** in Mexico with other Baptists from my church. Mission trips are trips that focus on volunteer work. This is my last mission trip as an eighth-grader. I wonder how different high school will be.

"I set the boxes over here!" I call to our group. Everyone nods. It's still morning, but we start early. We try to beat the heat when we can.

"Thanks, Maya." My friend Tim takes a break and wipes his brow. The sun beats down from a clear blue sky. It'll be another hot day today.

Find several Christian denomination churches in your area and look up their websites. Do they have activities or mission trips like Maya's? How are they reaching out to the community?

Tim and I both look back at the house we're building. "Can you believe there was nothing here just last month?" I ask him.

He shakes his head. "A lot of sweat went into that house."

"And faith," I say. This mission has been such a great experience for me. I actually get to help people! And the families are also here to help. They will be living in this house. They're so grateful.

Did you know? All Christians believe in baptism. Baptism is a sacred Christian ritual. Water is used to welcome the person into the community. Some baptize babies. Others, like Baptists, only baptize older children or adults.

"God's work," Jonah says as he passes us by with more lumber.

He's right, of course. Our church organized this trip last year. We did a fundraiser to pay for our travel expenses.

The outside of the house is up. Now we need to get the inside framed. Then there is electrical wiring and plumbing to do. Building a house is harder than I thought. "Isn't this the coolest thing you've ever done?" Tim asks me.

Did you know? Many Christians believe some people are gifted with speaking in tongues. This means they can speak a language they do not know. This gift comes from the Holy Spirit.

I nod. "Yes. I'm already thinking of coming back next year."

"Me too." Tim smiles.

"I know we're here to do God's work," I say. "But I feel good helping others. And I must admit, it's a little fun, too!" The mission trip is part of our belief, which includes helping those in need.

A group of little kids is laughing and jumping in the puddles. A parent shoos them away from the construction zone. It's exciting to think those families will be living in the houses we're building.

Jonah comes back with some bottles of water. "Stay hydrated, my friends."

We drink and take a break. Then it's back to work!

Do you help around your community or do volunteer work? How is it similar to Maya's trip? How is it different?

Did you know? Christian missionary work is more than volunteering. It is also about sharing the Christian faith.

CHAPTER 2
REFLECTING ON MISSION WORK

It was a long day of hard work. After we clean up, there's a meal of local fruits and vegetables. There's even freshly baked bread.

After we clean up the dinner mess, we sit by the campfire. Jonah picks up the guitar and starts strumming. We sing gospel songs. We talk about our day.

The local families join us for a couple songs. They even teach us a few songs in Spanish. They try to, at least. Some of those rolling Rs are so hard to pronounce! But we continue to practice.

Jonah asks, "Any thoughts about the day?" He asks this every evening. We get to think about both the good parts and the bad.

"It was *soooo* hot," Tim says. We all laugh.

"That it was," Jonah says with a smile. "Anything else?"

"They'll have a place to live," my friend Willa says.

ICHTHYS SYMBOL

The simple outline of a fish is often used as a symbol by Christians. This is called ichthys (IK-thuhs). It is the Greek word for "fish." It refers to Jesus feeding his followers fish. It also refers to Jesus calling his followers "fishers of men."

We all agree. The flames from the fire light up everyone's faces.

"I think I see the world a little differently now," I say. I think of my home, my room, and my community. "We may speak different languages. But I can see the joy in their eyes."

Tim adds, "I feel like God works through me."

I didn't always like to go to church. It felt stuffy and boring when I was little. My youth group is great though. When we're back home in Mississippi, we volunteer. Sometimes we work at the local homeless shelter.

This mission trip makes me feel closer to my faith and to God.

Jonah plays the guitar, and we all sing "This Little Light of Mine."

Did you know? The ladybug is tied to Christianity. Its name comes from a European story. Pests were destroying crops. Farmers asked for Our Lady's help. Our Lady is another name for Jesus's mother. Then, a swarm of beetles helped. The farmers named them "beetles of Our Lady."

I sing loudest at my favorite lyric, "This little light of mine, I'm gonna let it shine."

My bones and muscles are so tired. But I love this mission trip and the work we do.

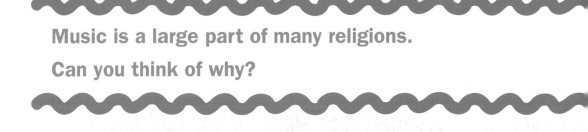

Music is a large part of many religions. Can you think of why?

David
German Catholic

CHAPTER 3
A YOUNG CATHOLIC IN GERMANY

"Mom, I'm so hungry," I complain as my stomach growls. Tomorrow is **Easter**. Easter is a holiday that celebrates Jesus rising from the dead. I'm looking forward to it. The **Mass** is long. But it makes me feel like it's a new beginning. Mass involves the celebration of the Eucharist, or Holy Communion. The Eucharist is a religious ritual where bread and wine become the Body and Blood of Jesus.

First there is Lent. Lent is a spiritual preparation before Easter. It's a time of sacrifice. This means we fast and give up things we like. This year, I'm giving up playing video games—for 40 days! But we don't fast on Sundays. This means I can play video games on Sunday. Phew!

Lent starts on Ash Wednesday. Ash Wednesday is a day of repentance. Repentance means asking forgiveness. Our priest sprinkled ashes on top of my head. My Catholic cousins in the United States get an ash cross on their foreheads on Ash Wednesday.

HOLIDAYS

Not all Christians observe the same holidays. Here are some holidays that could be part of a Christian's faith:

Advent: Celebrated in November and December. This holiday represents the beginning of the Christian year. It's also a preparation for celebrating the birth of Christ.

Christmas: A celebration on December 25 focused on the birth of Christ.

Lent: Celebrated late winter/early spring. Begins 40 days before Easter, on Ash Wednesday. Ash Wednesday is the start of Lent. Christians give up certain foods and fun activities to commemorate Jesus's suffering.

Easter: Celebration in spring, to remember Jesus's resurrection. Good Friday is the Friday before Easter, when Christ's crucifixion is remembered.

Did you know? Relics are holy objects. There are relics that are saints' fingernails and blood. There are even full body relics! Saint Bernadette's body is one. It is over 130 years old. It has not decomposed. Decompose means to breakdown.

Yesterday was Good Friday. Good Friday is when Jesus died on the cross. This is the only day all year when Mass isn't celebrated. We also fast on Good Friday. Because so many people are Catholic in Germany, it's a holiday. There is no school or work that day.

Now it's Saturday, and the 6 weeks of Lent have almost passed. I'm helping my mother in the kitchen.

"Pass me the flour, David," she says.

I'm happy to help. I look forward to being able to eat the bread tomorrow!

My older brother, Michael, gets the eggs from the fridge. "I'm getting hungry just looking at these."

"Remember why we fast, Michael," my mom says softly. But she smiles. We're all excited for Easter tomorrow.

Some people think Christmas is our biggest celebration. It's actually Easter. With Ash Wednesday and Lent, it's the most important remembrance of Jesus and his sacrifices.

My mom mixes the yeast with the flour, then the eggs and milk. The kitchen smells so nice.

We'll have to wait until Easter tomorrow to eat it!

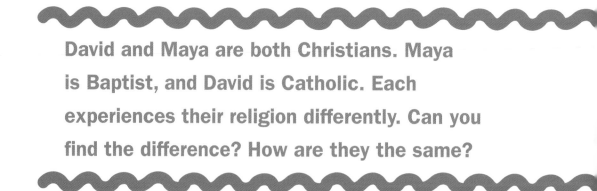

David and Maya are both Christians. Maya is Baptist, and David is Catholic. Each experiences their religion differently. Can you find the difference? How are they the same?

10 COMMANDMENTS

The Bible includes the 10 Commandments. They are considered moral guidelines. That means rules to live by.

1. Love God more than anything else.

2. Don't make anything in life more important than God.

3. Say God's name with love and respect.

4. Honor the Lord by resting on Sunday.

5. Love and respect your mother and father.

6. Do not kill.

7. Respect marriage promises.

8. Do not steal.

9. Tell the truth.

10. Do not be jealous of what others have.

Did you know? A patron saint is a saint whom Catholics ask for specific help. There is a patron saint of coffee. There is one of lost things. There is even one of the internet! Pictured is Saint Gertrude. She is the patron saint of cats.

CHAPTER 4
AN EASTER CELEBRATION

I wake up early on Sunday. It's Easter! I get dressed in my suit—my mom will be happy to see me dressed up. Then I meet my family, and we walk to church. I'm a little nervous. I sing in the choir. There will be a lot of people listening.

Everyone looks their best. The church is packed. I'm not surprised. Easter is one of my favorite holidays. So, I assume it's other Catholics' favorite, too!

Father Jacob does an excellent job with the homily. The homily is like a sermon. It is a talk that directly follows the reading of the Gospel. Father Jacob talks about the Crucifixion. I look at the crucifix hanging above the altar. It makes me think of Christ and his sacrifice.

After the homily, the choir sings. I'm a soprano. I get nervous for Easter. Once we start singing though, I forget about everything else.

We sing **hymns** with the choir. Hymns are religious poems or songs.

This Easter, we sing from the hymn book Gotteslob. Hymns are religious songs. We sing *"Den Herren will ich loben."* That means "I want to praise the Lord."

My friend Jurgen sighs with relief once we're done. "I was so nervous!"

I nod. "We sounded great, I think."

After the service, the choir meets in the back room of the church.

"Well done, young men," Father Jacob says. He smiles. "I'm very proud of you all."

Did you know? The father of the
Big Bang theory was a Catholic priest.

SACRED TEXTS

Christians follow the Bible as a sacred text. The Bible is a collection of writings from centuries ago. The Christian Bible is divided into the Old Testament and the New Testament.

The Old Testament is Jewish scriptures. It talks of God's creation of Earth and the rise and fall of Israel and Judah.

The New Testament tells the story of Jesus and his apostles. It also includes sacred letters and writings about the end of times.

I go to meet my family. Now, it's time to celebrate in town! There is an Easter parade, and we play egg toss and other games. Later, there's a bonfire. That's my favorite part. I get to hang out with my friends.

But first, we go home to eat. There's a big Easter feast. My mom is a great cook. All my aunts, uncles, and cousins join us. Easter is a family celebration for us.

I even get gifts for Easter. This year, I get a book, notebooks, and pencils. The bread we made with my mom turned out great.

Frohe Ostern! Happy Easter to all.

I'm off to the bonfire!

Both Maya and David sing to celebrate their faith. If you have a religion, is music part of it? Is it the same, or different?

ACTIVITY

PAINTING EASTER EGGS

Many people celebrate Easter by painting eggs. Eggs are often the symbol of a new beginning.

WHAT YOU NEED:

Eggs	Tongs
Saucepan	Vinegar
Bowl	Gloves
Food coloring	Brushes and paint
Plastic cups	

DIRECTIONS:

1. Boil the eggs in water in a saucepan for about 10 minutes. Carefully remove them using tongs.
2. Cool the eggs in a bowl of cold water. The eggs should be completely cooled before coloring.
3. Fill the plastic cups with water. Add 1 teaspoon (5 milliliters) of vinegar plus 1 teaspoon (5 mL) of food coloring.
4. Put your boiled eggs in each of the cups. Let stand for about 5 minutes.
5. Let the eggs dry completely. You can then use the brushes to paint any design on them.

TIMELINE of MAJOR EVENTS

4–6 BCE: Jesus is born

+/– 30 CE: Jesus is killed in Jerusalem

36: Paul, an important evangelist, becomes a Christian

150: The beliefs of Christians are stated in the Apostles, Creed

400: The New Testament is written and finished

1455: The Bible is first printed using a modern printing press

1517: German monk Martin Luther breaks away from the Catholic Church to start the Lutheran Church; this is the beginning of Protestantism

1609: John Smyth founds the Baptist Church

1729: John Wesley creates the Methodist Church, another Protestant branch

1948: The World Council of Churches is formed to unite Christians

2013: Pope Benedict XVI is the fifth Pope in history to resign; Pope Francis becomes Pope

2014: Pope John Paul II is canonized and recognized as a saint

LEARN MORE

FURTHER READING

Marsico, Katie. *Christianity.* Ann Arbor, MI: Cherry Lake Publishing, 2017.

Nardo, Don. *Christianity.* Mankato, MN: Compass Point Books, 2010.

Self, David. *The Lion Encyclopedia of World Religions.* Oxford, UK: Lion Children's, 2008.

WEBSITES

BBC Bitesize—What is Christianity?
https://www.bbc.co.uk/bitesize/topics/ztkxpv4/articles/zvfnkmn

Britannica Kids—Christianity
https://kids.britannica.com/kids/article/Christianity/352957

GLOSSARY

Christos (KRIH-stohs) in Greek, anointed or chosen one

clergy (KLUHR-jee) people ordained to perform services for a church

crucified (KROO-suh-fyed) put to death by nailing or binding the hands and feet to a wooden cross

Easter (EE-stuhr) a holiday that celebrates Jesus's resurrection

Holy Trinity (HOH-lee TRIH-nuh-tee) the Christian belief that God is the Father, the Son, and the Holy Spirit in one person

hymns (HIMS) religious songs

icon (EYE-kahn) an important figure

Mass (MASS) the celebration of the sacrament of Holy Communion

mission trip (MIH-shuhn TRIP) travels by church members to help others and spread their faith

monotheism (mah-nuh-THEE-ih-zuhm) the belief in one God

polytheism (PAH-lee-thee-ih-zuhm) the belief in multiple gods

rabbi (RAH-bye) Jewish teacher and leader

resurrected (reh-zuh-REK-tuhd) raised from the dead

INDEX

Advent, 20
Ash Wednesday, 19, 22

baptism, 11
Baptists, 8–17
Bible, 28, 31

Catholic Church, 7, 31
Catholics, 6, 7, 18–29
Christian populations, 5
Christianity
  beliefs, 6, 23
  branches and denominations, 6, 31
  history, 5–6, 31
  sacred texts, 28, 31
Christmas, 20
clergy, 6, 7, 25
communion, 19

Easter, 19, 20, 22, 25–26, 29, 30
Easter eggs, 30
Eucharist, 19

fasting, 19, 22

God, 6
Good Friday, 21

holidays, 19–22
holy communion, 19
holy objects, 21
Holy Spirit, 6, 12
holy trinity, 6

ichthys (fish) symbol, 16

Jesus Christ, 4–5, 19, 22, 25, 31
Judaism and Jews, 5, 28

ladybugs, 17
Lent, 19–21, 22

mass, 19, 25–26
missionary work, 9–17
monotheistic religions, 5
music, 16–17

New Testament, 28

Old Testament, 28

papal conclaves, 7
patron saints, 24
Peter (saint), 7
polytheism, 5
Popes, 6, 7, 31
Protestantism, 6, 9-17, 31

relics, 21
resurrection, 6, 19
rites and rituals, 11, 19

sacred texts, 28, 31
saints, 7, 24
speaking in tongues, 12

10 Commandments, 23
timeline, 31
trinity, 6

volunteer and mission work, 9–17

worship, 12, 19, 25–26